The Art of Conscious Manifestation

Feeling is the Secret
&
the Secret Feeling is Love

RITA CRAGWALL

ISBN: 9798725632729

DEDICATION

To the Son of God

Humanity

This is dedicated to each and every person out there who says
I AM

CONTENTS

PREFACE

There are all sorts of Principles that are also known as Laws. By definition they pass the Scientific Method. They are always working, work for all, and never deviate. If it deviates, then it is a rule. Rules are made to be broken.

Ex. Water goes to the lowest point - that is a principle of Newtonian Physics

Principle does not care who you are or what you have said or done as in they just don't give a caca one way or another. They are Principles. You are here to learn and the question is did you learn something?

Humanity as a whole is the Son of God and each one of us is the Son of God individually and everyone knows all things are possible to God. We are fractals of God - Consciousness.

The word God means I AM aka Consciousness aka Awareness of Being.

Science has shown us we have a brain - consciousness - in our hearts. Each one of us has it and it is the first thing made - these neurons, this brain, this consciousness - when the sperm and egg hook up. Then the heart is made and then the spine and then the brain - a clean consciousness with one side all clean and the other side a clean purse and your brother/mother who sits between the two sides of the whole. That is your consciousness, subconscious - a sub part of the consciousness (the purse), and your imagination - the pineal gland.

It's One Consciousness and the Subconscious is part of the consciousness. The subconscious has that feeler - nerve - that connects the two consciousnesses. The one in your heart keeps you alive and functioning. It heals you when you cut yourself. It tells you when you are hungry and need food and thirsty for water. It is your intuition, it is your guide. It guides you and presents something to your consciousness.

All hearts and all imaginations are connected and speak to each via feeling aka vibration. The frequency of that vibration is the passion and intensity that you feel something.

You may see 100 cars in the day but only one catches your eye - your love - your attention.

You fill up your purse - your subconscious - with the things you have given attention to and to the things you have consciously accepted as true in life. The things you respond to is all you. You are to be responsible for your response. You are to understand that everyone else is responding to your vibration and vice versa.

If you dislike what others are saying or doing then be responsible - go within and change it - change what you are aware of and the world outside you changes. It's all within.

As within - so without.

You are born with a clean consciousness and the one in your heart is guiding you and thinking for you disguised as you and your imagination is spinning stories based off your feelings and the images you automatically evoke when you speak or think.

We all do it and we know we all do it. It's all a story we all make up and feed with the secret behind the secret.

You are the Child of God and you are here to learn how to use your power and when you don't use it properly you are forced to face your monsters and you can't get rid of them until you use your power properly. Principle is no respecter of persons. It works for all regardless of who you think you are - no one is better than or less than another.

The secret is it's all feeling. emotion and the secret feeling behind the secret is love. That is your power - Consciousness and Love.

The universe isn't doing a thing other than being the best universe it can be. It is the created not the creator. It is not aware of being. It does not imagine. It does not say I AM. You do. The art of consciously manifestation is learning how to use your power. Feeling is the secret and the secret feeling is Love.

I hope this helps you learn how to use your power - the power of love - the power of your unconditional love - attention.

ACKNOWLEDGMENT

Sincere thanks and appreciation and love to the Followers of the Way who support this message and the way I present it.

Ann Bergman, Anna, Apollo Sam, Avrill Weinman, Bahayan Destinations, Bettina, Charles Tanedo, Chee, Christine Wesson, Cindy Williams, Claudio Peña Aguilar, Ema. Emma Louise Rowe. Eryn. Esther. Gail Marie MacLean. Gini. Grace. Hannah. Jacqueline Cox. Jenn Blais. Jennifer. Julie O'Donnell, Kitty Tripp, Kristine Offutt, Kyle Shortal, Lef To, Libby Patterson, Mariyah Raza, Mark Young, Matthew Weaver, Michael Heath, Mohana, Patty Hawley, Rachael O'Meara Curran, Rachelle Reynolds, Ruby, Suzanne Sanderson, Tina, V K, and many more.

I am honored & blessed to serve them!

1 LOVE IS THE ONLY POWER

The word God is a Greek translation and it means in ancient Hebrew Awareness of being - Consciousness and the Human Imagination.

The characters in the Bible that never lived represent Humanity and each one of us individually.

The name Moses means to draw out and Moses is a Man. He goes up the holy mountain. Mountains represent your mind and the holy mountain is when you go within after silencing your mind. He goes into his head and meditates and thinks what is God? He is shown a bush on fire that does not burn - that comes straight out of Man's imagination. Then he hears - I am THAT - I AM which means I am drawn out of Man's imagination - I am - Awareness of being. God presents to Man what Man is aware of being in his imagination - his perception of himself and his perception of others.

God is Consciousness and he draws out of Man's imagination what Man is Aware of and gives his love and attention to in his imagination. This is then presented to Man. God is the Father and his son is Man's Imagination. Man is the Observer, God is the only Power. God is Love. Love conquers all.

God is deaf, dumb, blind. He cannot taste, smell or see. He feels. He is in your heart as science has shown us. He feels you. He feels what you feel. Imagination cannot speak. It sees, hears, tastes, smells, and feels. You speak. You are the operator of them. You have dominion over all. You have the five senses and you feel and your words evoke your imagination and feelings - automatically.

The common denominator is feeling and the secret feeling is love.

Love binds it all up and presents it to you and you are to love it. You feel and you speak words and they evoke images and feelings you associated with them and the word brings images to imagination and the feeling is sent to the Consciousness in your heart and he loves you so he always says yes.

Your word always comes back to you so you can see what you have created in your mind and manifested in this place. So you can see what you believe - what you are conscious of.

Proponents of the Secret and the Law of Attraction think manifesting comes from the universe. This is a misunderstanding and a failure to comprehend what is being read and what is actually happening when one manifests. We all do it all the time.

There are 12 Laws of Mind and Law of Attraction proponents mush them up all into one - leaving out the most important one - and call it the Law of Attraction. They don't comprehend the Law of Attraction either. They think they are vibrating the same frequency as 'money' or a 'house' or a special person by thinking of them.

They are missing the mark completely. Many do not comprehend what they are reading. The word sin means missing the mark. Hit the target instead of missing the mark.

These are universal laws - not laws of the universe - principle. It doesn't matter what universe you are in - these universal laws are principle. Principle of Mind. As long as you think and say I AM they are in play. Without you there are no Principles of Mind.

In other words, they are the nature of your being.

As such, proponents perpetuate this falsehood it's the universe doing it and it grows and then the day comes when they ask - is the universe mad at me?

The universe is not doing a thing. It's just being the best universe it can be. These are universal laws not laws of the universe.

The word God in ancient Hebrew and/or Greek means Consciousness - Awareness of being. The universe is not aware of being. It does not say I AM and it does not feel nor imagine. You do with God.

God aka Consciousness is a being without form or shape and it is the human imagination that shapes God into all these forms we see - including ourselves. HE is a Being. He laughs and cries and that is where laughter and tears come from. An explosion of love from your heart.

Love binds it up and presents it to Man to experience so he learns how to think - like his Father - God in his heart.

Human Beings are blessed to express life and experience what they express.

EVERYTHING and EVERYONE is made from God and all of it is made by the human imagination.

Human beings have two consciousnesses and they choose which one to be in charge. There is one in the head and we are learning to think with it and the one in our hearts that guides us and teaches us how to think.

There is a consciousness in our hearts. It is whole and pure and it guides us. The Bible speaks of this and science has proven there is a brain in our hearts - neurons - whole and complete - it is not split in two - it has no subconscious.

God is a being without form. His Son - Imagination - is a being without form. Imagination shapes God into the forms and God gives it Life - presents it to Man's consciousness. They formed Man and take form in him and everything else.

Man is the Great Judge. He is to learn to err on the side of Love for God is Love and is the only power. Attention is unconditional love. Law of Attraction is like thoughts/beliefs attract like circumstances, conditions, events and people into your life. If you think about something or someone then you are giving it unconditional love - attention. You will be given THAT!

Ex. You may hate racism but it is you thinking of it, feeding it - giving it attention - no matter which side you are on. It's a good intention and good intentions pave the road to hell. If you hate it then someone has to play the role you hate as you gave it attention - your love. You are the one loving on it. If you do not change your thoughts eventually you become what you hate so you can walk in their shoes and learn. Forgive them for showing you THAT and forget it and it will leave your life. Up to you of course. It's your life.

The Bible is to be read subjectively so you understand these truths.

God is a Being but he can't be seen. Man was created - he did not think. Then Man was given a mind. As such Man can't comprehend God unless He is presented through allegory, and parable. God is a being without form and it is his Son the human imagination that shapes him into various forms for Man to see. It's a story so Man will learn and will rewrite the story to be as he wishes. Science calls it a lucid dream. Science states you can take charge in lucid dreams. You can be free. You can take charge.

Man was made before the Universe. He is the vessel these two work through. Without observation - there is nothing. Unless you see, hear, taste, smell, touch it in your imagination there is no-thing.

This is why allegories are used to explain God so Man can comprehend it, associate things with it and understand it. He can't get the concept without that.

When you say that God is Love it must mean what love means when applied to human beings. As we evolve we come to understand God IS Love. The love a parent for their child, the love of a spouse, the crab that loves it's babies, the love of beauty, art, music, entertainment - love in all it's flavors.

The Secret is in the feeling and the secret feeling is love.

The love of God for each one of us is like the love of a mother for her child, or the love of the musician for his instrument or his music. The love of a pet.

God is love and God is life.

The secret is in the feeling and the secret feeling is love.

Many people say that God is Love and at the same time believe He hands out eternal damnation for our actions. The word sin in the Bible means missing the mark. You wish to be something and you think things or people on the outside have to do it for you or stop you from having it in some way. You wish to be rich but you are not. You wish to be healthy but you are not. You are missing the mark. You see life objectively - that is sin. You are missing the mark.

To sin is to believe the outside world - you believe what others say and we are told things by others and we come to think for example we can't have a career without a degree or that we are less than those who do have degrees. We all do it. Hence the statement we are all sinners.

Many claim that God is just, and yet believe that people living today are suffering poverty or disabilities for a sin supposed to have been committed by Adam thousands of years before they were born.

Adam is part of the dream that the one Man is having while he dreams the dream of becoming one with God. Adam represents Humanity and each one of us individually. That original sin is seeing life objectively vs subjectively. That is our journey. We are going home the long way around.

God and his Son want you to join them in expressing life forever and so you have to learn. You are expressing life and you get to experience what you express so you learn. God put Man to sleep and now you journey. You are the Prodigal Son.

That 'original' sin is you are a victim of circumstance rather than a victim of your own thinking that brings those circumstances into play in your life.

This means victim brownie points are uncool and is actually being a bully. You did it to yourself. A bully is merely a victim overcompensating and you believe in them so you get to experience them as that is what you are expressing in your life and the price you pay for your beliefs is you get to experience them and then become them so you can experience the whole of it.

When you split love in two you get good and bad. You will experience both until you learn. Love brings it together.

There are some people who believe that every human being was predestined to heaven or hell before he was created, and that his conduct, good or bad while on this earth, would make no difference to his fate in life.

You are God's Child and therefore you are predestined to walk your road and learn and this was laid out before you were born. A perfect life has been planned for each individual. It is up to each individual to accept that or not and let Imagination bring it to you.

Baptize means to be immersed in. When you are born you come out of a womb of water. You are baptized in water - into this physical world and you are baptized in fire - the circumstances, conditions, events and people that come into your life for you to experience what you express about life in your consciousness and imagination. All of this is so you the child will learn how to think.

You are predestined to walk through this hell and then reach heaven. Baptized in fire. You are predestined to get to heaven. Each one of us in our own way walks through hell and gets to heaven. That is what is predestined. How you do that is up to you of course.

All for One and One for All - no human being is left behind.

Humanity is a divine being - God's Child - and therefore so is each human being that makes up Humanity. You can't know good until you know bad. Welcome to Hell aka Boot Camp aka School.

The character you wear - Tom, Mary, Julie - consists of your thoughts and beliefs. The sum total of these is what you vibrate - Law of Vibration - and in turn you attract the circumstances, conditions, events and people that come into your life - Law of Attraction.

Therefore your beliefs are your fate. You are in charge of it. You have dominion over all here. All beliefs are self imposed and are represented in the Bible as the fish of the deep. You can throw it back. You can change beliefs and indeed we do it all the time and in turn your fate is changed.

As within so without. The one Principle in the outside world is things are always changing. Always.

God **is** Love, Life, and Intelligence. He works with perfect wisdom and perfect justice for all, at all times. Justice is to err on the side of love - always.

"God is light, and in Him is no darkness at all" - I John 1:5

God does not authorize 'bad' or 'negative'. It does not exist really. We make that caca up and then wallow in it like a pig that wallows in mud.

The ancient Greeks did not have one word for love. They had three: eros, erotic or sexual love; philio, brotherly love, and agape, spiritual love.

The Bible notes all three, but focuses on brotherly love and instructs man to understand and express spiritual love. It teaches that what you think of when having a physical act of love - sex - that - whatever it was - is presented to you in some way.

16 So we know and believe the love God has for us. God is love, and he who abides in love abides in God, and God abides in him.
I John 4:16

To abide means to live. There is nothing more important than love.

God is love. Love is Power. Love is by far the most important thing of all. It is the common denominator in all of life.

To pray is to be by yourself, talking to yourself, going into your head and to think upon something with feeling. Attention is unconditional love and the secret to manifesting is the feeling of love - love conquers all - even unto death.

We pray all the time. There are many ways to pray for prayer is thinking when you are alone or in your head. Meditation is one of the best ways to pray but misunderstood. To think of something and ponder on it is meditating on something. Pray for the understanding of love, and think about it - meditate - daily. Fear cannot exist in the presence of love.

Nothing 'bad' can happen in the presence of love. All must respond in kind to love. That is principle at work.

Love casts out fear. Love conquers all sin - thinking objectively and all the caca that brings. Love is absolutely invincible. It is THE Super Hero within.

There is no problem that enough love will not fix. There is no mountain so big that love cannot remove it. There is no illness that enough love will not heal. There is no door that enough love will not open.

There is no sin that enough love will not redeem.

It makes no difference what the trouble may be, how impossible it may seem, or how great the mistake - love conquers all.

Love will dissolve and change it all. If you could love enough you would be the happiest and most powerful being in the world.

Statements like Love Never Fails or Love Solves Every Problem or Love Conquers All are often made by people who say they believe them but do not in their hearts. God sits in your heart and he knows if you mean it or not.

They think they are little and insignificant. They think of Love as some sort of Power outside themselves that has to be earned instead of felt and appreciated. In turn they believe, due to this low self-esteem, that if they beg hard enough, this Power will come down and rescue them. As a rule they will not admit they believe such an idea, but that is what they are actually entertaining in their minds.

There is, in fact, no such outside power, and therefore you cannot receive help in that way. God is not ignoring you - you just aren't talking to him.

In 1991 science discovered a 'brain in our hearts.

That is a consciousness and the word God means consciousness. God is in your own heart as the Bible states over and over.

If you want it all - all the time - then the thing for you to do is to fill your own heart with Love, by thinking about it, feeling it, and expressing it; and when this sense of Divine Love is vivid enough it will heal you and solve your problems, and it will enable you to heal others too. That is the Law of One aka the Law of Being.

If your mother is sick and you sit down and go within and imagine your father saying your mom is perfectly fine and you say thank you and repeat that over and over and hold that feeling of love and relief that your mom who you love is perfectly fine and that feeling fills you up and explodes out of your solar plexus then your prayer for your Mom was successfully launched and she will be perfectly fine. Miracles happen all the time.

Now we can see why sarcasm, grumbling, holding grudges, thinking one is less than or better than another, the desire to compete against others rather than self, maligning the color of another's skin instead of getting to know what is in their head, coveting what others have, etc., are fatal because they prevent Divine Love from healing us - making us whole.

Affirm this often and it will change your life. Say it slowly and with feeling - mean it when you say it. At first you won't mean it when you say it because you are in a bad habit. Keep it up - persist - and God in your heart will bring you understanding and that feeling of love will fill your body, mind and soul.

God IS Love and God is Life and he always says yes. God only wishes to express love and life and it is Man who expresses life through his words and feelings those words evoke. The actual words don't matter - it is the feeling of love behind the words that matter. Your imagination is automatically engaged when you speak.

My soul is filled with Divine Love. I am surrounded by Divine Love. I radiate Love, Peace and good will to the whole world without distinction. God is Love, and there is nothing in existence but God and His Self-expression. All men are expressions of God - Divine Love; therefore, I can meet with nothing but the expressions of Divine Love. All must respond in Love. Nothing ever takes place but the Self-expressing of Divine Love. This is Divine Truth. I do not have to try to bring this about. I observe it already in being - now. Divine Love is the actual true nature of Being. There is only Divine Love, and I know this.

I perfectly understand what Divine Love is. I have a conscious realization of Divine Love. The Love of God burns in me for all humanity, I am a lamp of God, radiating Divine Love to all whom I meet, to all whom I think of.

I forgive everything that can possibly need forgiveness - absolutely everything. Divine Love fills my heart, and all is well. I now radiate Love to the whole universe, excluding no one. I express Divine Love. I experience Divine Love.   I thank God for this.

If you express love - then you get to experience it too.

This prayer comes from Emmett Fox and using this prayer as a daily exercise will help you find peace and happiness. Change the words to make it work for you if you wish. It works perfectly and is a beautiful little prayer that takes care of it all once it sinks in. Persist in saying it and eventually the meaning of it sinks in.

Each one of us is different and so there are many roads to the same end. That end? To jettison out of here and do what we were always meant to do - to receive the Promise - to grow up. To express life.

Humanity is the Word come to Life.

The shortest and easiest pathway of all is the Pathway of Love.

Love is the common denominator, the simplest of all the paths, and it is the most direct, efficient, and the easiest too.

It is the one pathway which is open to all, everywhere, regardless of conditions or surrounding circumstances.

Love stands for something much bigger and finer and more powerful than any mere personal opinion.

Love is the motivation, the power in Consciousness, and it is the quality of Love that leads it to seek to expand for fuller and fuller expression, for Love must be expressed. That is rising up in Consciousness.

The principal aspects of God is Life, Truth and Love.

Life is existence, and this is the Truth of Being. Life must express itself and Love is the perfect expression of Life. In other words, what we call Love is really the full and unrestricted expression of Divine Life itself. That is why it always means perfect peace, perfect wholeness, perfect beauty, perfect joy and why Jesus said,

"I am come that they might have Life, and that they might have it more abundantly." - John 10:10

Jesus is the representation of the son of God - the Savior. He is the human imagination, yours and everyone else's - who shape love and life into all it's various forms and aspects according to what the human being imagines and believes in their hearts where God lays.

The mummies of ancient times were made in such a way to represent that Man is a Vessel - they empty the organs out of the body.

God in our hearts gets wrapped up in layers and when you peel them off you get the heart of gold that shines in man. So they wrapped the body up in layers and preserved his body. This was a vessel for the Divine.

Then the burial places are filled with their story and what they did and the riches and beauty they enjoyed. The body is then locked away - locked into the minds of men and therefore God.

These burials were a celebration of life as expressed by XXX. All burials all. It's not the date or birth or death that matters - it's that dash in between them that matters.

Pyramids are not burial sites. Not one body has been found in any pyramid. They are the ancient means of lighting up the world that Man has yet to figure out.

We forgot along the way and started making up stories about them according our perceptions.

Now we see why the opposite of Love is fear; and why fear is the supreme enemy of mankind. Everybody knows this today. Stress is fear and we all know stress makes us ill and enough stress kills.

Science is about taking the fear out of life. It also takes the love out of it. Two sides to the coin.

There is nothing to fear but fear itself.

Fear is the absence of Love.

"Fear hath torment but perfect Love casteth out fear" I John 4:18.

The only reason we have any fear at all is because we do not love God enough. A great mystic said, "Love God and do what you please," knowing that with the love of God in our hearts our expression could only be perfect. A modern seer has told us, "You can get rid of any difficulty whatever from your life as soon as you can love God more than you love the error."

Love is attention. Give your love to God rather than to your Fear.

Anger, spite, resentment, racism, hate etc., the negative, are expressions of fear. Jealousy, malice, and "all uncharitableness" indicates a fear of not enough to go around - lack of - and if the other fellow gets all that he wants of 'good', we shall have to go without. This is a lack of mentality and it is fear talking and blocks the expression of Life.

This thinking is an absence of Love for self and is reflected in life.

Condemnation, resentment, maligning, are chains upon the free flow of Life. They are limitations, restrictions, congestion or blocks and since it exists in the minds of human beings then it shows up as sin - sickness, poverty, ignorance, and death. Maligning creates malignancies aka cancer. You may do as Objective Man says and defeat that cancer by almost killing yourself to do it but if you don't change the way you think you will get more. Science calls that metastasized cancer.

Men and women grow old, and tired, and wrinkled, and worn, and ultimately lose their bodies altogether. The earth is desolated by wars, and famine, and pestilence - greed and corruption.

Thus we begin to see the reason why the Bible has always laid so much stress upon the outstanding importance of Love. Unless we build up within our own minds and hearts a real and practical Love-consciousness, aka the Christ Consciousness, our activities will be more or less useless.

If we have the Love-consciousness well developed toward all - everything else will follow. No need to worry about anything on the outside. It is all taken care of.

The art of consciously manifesting life is the Pathway of Love which is open to everyone in all circumstances, and which you may step up to at any moment and requires no formal education, no entrance exam. All are welcome.

You begin by refusing to accept any negative thought.

Begin to lose the thought of personal condemnation aka judging and maligning others. It's just a person. You don't condemn the person - you condemn their thinking. If they change their thinking you welcome them back. This is the story of the Prodigal Son we are all living all the time.

Throw away resentment for old injuries, and of everything which is contrary to Love via forgiveness. You must not allow yourself to hate either person, or group, institution or nation, or anything whatsoever.

You must build up by consistent daily exercise the true Love consciousness, and then all the rest of life follows.

Life follows you. What you know in your heart - you get. That is the law of vibration and the law of attraction. They are principles and you can't escape principle. You vibrate the sum total of your state of consciousness and you attract what you vibrate. What you feel to be true in your heart.

Love washes all sin away. Love will heal you. Love will comfort you. Love will guide you. Love will bring you understanding and intelligence. Love will redeem you from sin, sickness,poverty, and death, and lead you into the promised land, the place that is altogether lovely.

Love requires no equipment beyond the readiness to practice it, yet that readiness is likely to cost so much in the way of effective self-sacrifice that those who truly seek it are few.

Love is the fastest way to end all your individual difficulties, and because your mind is part of the mind of humanity, it is actually the quickest way in which you can raise up Humanity too.

It is the one path that is open for everyone to enter, at any moment. The plain man earning a modest living in a restaurant or store can practice the Path of Love wherever he finds himself.

The only question is whether one is really willing to pay the price - is really prepared to put God first. Is really prepared to love God with all his heart, mind and being.

Divine love is not something to think about only. It must be in your heart - wrapped around it - a knowing. It must be expressed in daily life not just pondering on it.

An example from Neville Goddard of this was a woman who every day bought a paper and took it to an elderly neighbor. They would spend a little time each day together having some company and enjoying each other. The elderly lady passed and a few days later this woman learned all this lady had possessed was left to her and it was indeed a fortune. This woman made a point of making sure one who was lonely had some company each day and it came from her heart. It was sincere and no thought of reward for doing it.

Yet she was rewarded. She had embraced the love of God and each day when she woke up she would say I am a wealthy woman - I have XXX in the bank. Then she went out and loved on life - this lonely elderly lady.

Her love for this woman was the key to those riches coming to her. She had no idea and none of us do - so be aware.

Love is always working, always providing, always growing through you.

Love conquers all.

2 PRAYER

There is only one way to change the outside world. It comes from within and the power is Love that does it and that is a feeling inside man that he associates with people, events, places, conditions, circumstances. Man's attention.

It is Principle that man will attract the conditions, circumstances, people, events, that he has taken on to be true. What he has given his love to - his attention. These things go into your purse - the subconscious mind. They make their way to the consciousness in your heart if given enough attention and once it is wrapped around the heart then it comes to be true in the individual's consciousness.

There is no other way. This is how manifestation works.

Now you can try to do this yourself but that is the hard way - the human way. It is much easier to call upon that power within you to do it for you. Prayers is how you do that. Whether you realize it or not you are always praying.

Mankind is always seeking a hack - a short cut of some kind or other because the consciousness in your head aka the objective mind is lazy. However there is hack available and Man knows this in his heart which is why he seeks that hack. It is prayer.

Sadly the lazy man takes on the most pain in the long run, and having wasted his time in wandering this way or that way, listening to others rather than to the one in his heart - he is ultimately driven by failure, pain and suffering to the realization of the truth that there is no substitute for love.

The way to use love as your sword and shield is through prayer. Prayer is your Batman utility belt.

When humans have exhausted all other avenues then they turn to prayer. It can't hurt and maybe it will help.

Prayer is not repeating a 'prayer' in some building someone told you to say. If you can't say it with feeling and understanding then it can't help you. That is not praying. That is begging and no one is listening to that.

Prayer is when you silence your mind - the consciousness in your head - and it is then you speak to the one behind the mask - the one in your heart. When you are in great pain or emotion that is the one that is being spoken to. When you are by yourself thinking or in your head thinking - even in a crowd - that is prayer.

There is nothing more powerful than prayer and we all do it all the time whether we realize it or not. Take control of your prayers and know what you are doing as you are praying all the time.

The first step is to find the natural way, the best way for you, the individual. Only you know how you talk to yourself and that is how you do it - how you pray.

First you go to silence and this is key. To go to silence is to silence the consciousness in your head where all the caca resides. There are many methods to choose from to go to silence.

Do a mundane task, riding the bus, riding in a car, in a crowd, walking, running, painting, dancing, singing, music, any creative work, motorcycle maintenance, sitting in a comfy chair, laying in the grass, kneading dough, drinking a glass of wine or beer, having a smoke.

Get relaxed and silence the mind in your head that spins the stories.

Going to silence is getting into the groove, it's feeling the beat, it's gelling, it's spacing out, it's getting into the vortex, it's the zone. You do it all the time.

Then spin your story. Weave your tale. Do it with great feeling and emotion. The I AM you are using at that time is the one in your heart - God. Be sincere - that method actor. Redo that scene you did not like. Die to that old man and become the new man. The Phoenix rising.

Ex. I go sit on the back porch and light a cigarette. I inhale it and blow it out not thinking just being. Then I say to myself - I did not hear Mary say Joe was sick with cancer. I heard Mary say Joe's physical came back and he is perfect! Bones of a thirty year old! She looks so happy! Amen to that!

You die to the old man that believed Joe was sick and became the new man that knows Joe is perfectly fine. Do not allow anything to interfere with what you have declared to be in consciousness. Revise it as soon as possible and Joe will heal.

Create a scene that indicates you or another won the golden ticket.

Be whatever you wish to be and your imagination will send that down to God in your heart if given with feeling - love. God always says yes. God IS life and sends it back up to you for your imagination to present to you wrapped up in your beliefs.

If you are confident it never fails. If you doubt it then you are double minded and it will be delayed and enough doubt will abort it.

Father and Son don't get 'bad'. That's all you. Your imagination will show you that bad you put in your head so you can get rid of it. His job is to tempt you with the desire God sends you and then to plot a course through your beliefs to give it to you once you accept it in your heart. It comes wrapped up in your beliefs. He must obey whichever consciousness you choose for him to obey. The one in your head or the one in your heart - your choice. He doesn't care one way or another. He loves you and gives you whatever you think about.

You get your desire wrapped up in your beliefs so you will change them and in the end lose them all but the knowing it is all you, your thinking, your imagination, and God in your heart doing all of this. You lose them all as the Bible tells us in the book of Exodus.

Practice forgiveness and love conscientiously every day. Look into the mirror into your eyes and say I love you. State daily I forgive all without distinction. Remove blocks aka congestion that stops love - the power from your heart - from flowing freely into all areas of your life.

Having chosen your method, set to work on some perceived problem in your life, choosing preferably whichever is causing you the most pain. I believe it is best to address whatever it is that you are most afraid of as that usually washes the rest away.

Remember, there is always a way out; that is as sure as the rising of the sun each morning. The problem really is, not the getting rid of your difficulties, but the finding of your own way of praying.

They were called Followers of the Way. Only one way - yours.

3 GOD SANDWICH - EFFECTIVE PRAYER

If illness is your difficulty, do not rest until you have brought about at least one physical healing in yourself or others. There is no illness that has not been healed by someone through prayer at some time, and what others have done you can do, for God is Love and Love is Pure Power and Principle, and Principle does not change - it is constant.

If poverty is the trouble then go to work on that, and clear it up once and for all. It can be done.

If you are unhappy, dissatisfied with your current situation in life, or your surroundings, or with yourself, work on that. Refuse to take "no" for an answer; and insist upon the happiness and satisfaction that are yours by Divine Right.

Claim your birthright with confidence. You are the Child of God and it is his pleasure to give you the kingdom. He always says yes. God is the Consciousness in your heart and he works with the Human imagination - his son that was once divine and became human to help mankind rise up and join them in expressing love and life.

If your need is a purpose - artistic, literary, or otherwise or if your heart's desire is to attain fame or recognition in a profession, or some kind of public career, that is perfectly fine and is a legitimate and worthy road. God sends you the desires. Accept them.

Someone has to play that role and if you would love to do that - whatever that is - then it is right for you.

The right method of Prayer will bring you the prize.

Avoid making excuses for not taking the time to pray. There are no excuses for failing to receive your desires in life. When you do not have your desires in life then it is only that you have not worked long enough or in the right way. Excuses are the devil who comes to tempt you to remain outside the Kingdom of Heaven, while the Gate stands open. Excuses are the only enemy that you really need to fear.

Find the method that resonates with you and that feels natural. Cultivate simplicity - simplicity and spontaneity are the secret of effective prayer. Tell no one what you are doing and work away steadily. Whatsoever ye shall ask in My name, that will I do.

His name? I AM.

Effective prayer is to tell yourself a story with feeling and then drop it. Not thinking of it again. Simple and spontaneous. Keep It Simple Spontaneous - KISS.

The objective of prayer is to produce a certain state of mind. That state of mind constitutes a true understanding concerning the problem in question and freedom from fear in connection with it. When this state of mind is impressed upon the consciousness in our hearts - the wish must show itself to you. You play at being rich in your mind, hearing others congratulate you etc. until it reveals itself to you. Play and drop it. Like a child. Play and drop it. Play and drop it until it is in your consciousness.

Whatever produces the required state of mind is a good way of prayer. Repeating certain affirmations, reading certain verses in the Bible, dancing to music, painting or writing it out or any other "method" of producing that state of mind is a good prayer method.

Then there is the God Sandwich. Sit in my comfy chair or go outside and weed the garden or go to the bathroom. Read a little of the Bible or spiritual book or writer you may enjoy, close your eyes, think of God, then claim it with thanks.

Ex. Thank you Father for changing how I see XXX - my financial situation, my physical health etc. I forgive everyone and everything that ever made me think that. I am now claiming my birthright. I am XXX. Thank you for taking my fear away from me. Thank you for helping me see there is always XXX. Thank you Sweet Jesus for saving me.

Then acknowledge who does do it and hand it over to them dropping it.

Ex. I know I don't do it. I know you do it. Thank you Sweet Jesus. Thank you Father. I know you hear me. I know you always hear me and I know you always say yes. Thank you!

Then think of God and the aspects of God.

A couple of my students call this a God Sandwich and it has stuck with me as the perfect name for this type of prayer.

This is a very effective form of prayer. Play when you do mundane tasks always ending with yeah that would be great - oh well you never know - effectively dropping it.

Each one of us is differently so you do have to find your own way.

Many sincere people have come to mistake the means for the end and think that praying mechanically or doing certain techniques makes it happen but this is not so. It must be sincere and it must have feeling behind it and that feeling is love.

Jesus cautions about vain repetitions. A vain repetition is saying something over and over without feeling.

Here is one way of solving a problem by Prayer.

Get by yourself, and be quiet for a few moments. This is very important. You must shut off the consciousness in your head so you can speak to the one in your heart. Just be quiet. Remind yourself that the Bible says *Be still, and know that I am (is) God.*

Then begin to think about God. Remind yourself of some of the things that you know about Him - that God is Life and that He is present everywhere, that He has all power, that He knows you and loves you and cares for you, etc., etc., etc. Read a few verses of the Bible, or a paragraph from any spiritual book that helps you.

During this stage it is important not to think about your problem, but to give your attention - your love - to God. In other words, do not try to solve your problem directly which would be forcing it but rather become interested in thinking of the nature of aka the aspects of God.

Then claim the thing that you wish to experience - a healing, or some particular good which you lack. Claim it quietly and confidently; as you would claim something to which you know is yours and you are entitled to it.

Then give thanks for the accomplished fact as you would if somebody handed you a gift.

"When you pray believe that you receive and you shall receive"
Matt. 21:22

Jesus in the Bible represents the human imagination. He represents a man who has obtained the state of Consciousness of One who Walks with God. You have this consciousness inside you. Rise up.

If you understood the Truth so well, then you know by merely giving thanks with sincere feeling for the accomplished fact makes it happen. Some call this the law of assumption. It is the knowing - the belief written on your heart - that God does it and you love God and are thankful for all he gives to you as he always gives to you and never says no.

For instance, in the feeding of the five thousand at the Sermon on the Mount he kept giving thanks for the supply, and the loaves and fishes kept multiplying. In the raising of Lazarus he said, "Thank thee Father for having heard me," and Lazarus came out of the tomb.

Do not discuss your prayers with anyone. Try not to be tense or hurried. Tension and hurry delay the demonstration. You know that if you try to unlock a door in a hurry, the key is apt to stick, whereas if you do it slowly, it moves easily.

If the key sticks, the thing is to stop pressing, and release it gently. To push hard with will power will only jam the lock completely.

It's the same in all things. In quietness and confidence shall be your strength. I have heard people say, "I did not pray when such a problem came up. I just knew the Truth about it, did not accept it and the trouble disappeared." This is exactly what effective prayer is, and in its most beautiful and effective form. You know the Imagination shapes it and the Consciousness in your heart does it. That's it.

Such a person means that he has not used some rigid technique of prayer, which, needless to say, is not in the least required. You don't have to do any of them and there are many - state akin to sleep, tea ceremony, scripting to name a few.

Techniques help when you don't have enough faith. They help you build faith. If you continue to use the techniques after years of receiving in this way then you are giving the technique power and it will fail you eventually. Belief is not required. You learn your faith is all that is required.

Techniques are great and something to fall back on when spontaneity fails. Then they help to focus the thought, and set the stage. But - the thought's the thing and the simpler and more spontaneous it is, the more quickly it comes. This is how we do it unconsciously. Now flip it and do the same thing only consciously. Only you know how you talk to yourself and what that spontaneous type of imagining might be.

To know the Truth is really to know yourself and that the problem in question does not belong to you as a child of God. It 's unbecoming of a divine being.

You have an angel in your heart taking care of the everything.

Many people actually do all their prayer with formal statements of Truth, and get consistently good results by praying in this way. Not through repeating affirmations like a parrot. Those who pray like a parrot inevitably remain in the cage.

One who prays in this manner uses the same phrases or affirmations many times but he fills them with fresh feeling every time.

Each prayer must be as fresh as the morning dew.

For one whose intuition is not strong nor has the ability to easily express his thoughts in words, using affirmations is a great way to pray.

Over time your intuition will strengthen and grow. You can and really should make a special point of praying for a strong intuition regularly every day - claiming it, of course.

I have conscious Divine Intelligence. I individualize the Infinite. I have direct knowledge of Truth. I have perfect intuition. I have spiritual perception. I know.

It is your intuition that guides you on your journey in life and takes you to the things you have prayed for in life.

40

4 FAITH

21 And Jesus answered them, "Truly, I say to you, if you have faith and never doubt, you will not only do what has been done to the fig tree, but even if you say to this mountain, 'Be taken up and cast into the sea,' it will be done. - Matthew 21:21

An understanding of faith is the life of prayer. Your belief is not required - your faith is required.

Faith is knowing the unseen will be seen. Everyone knows any team can beat any other team on any given day. That is faith. The question is - how strong is your faith?

It is a great mistake to struggle to produce a strong faith within yourself. That can only end in failure as it is not sincere.

When you are unsure of your faith - you don't feel like you can assume it will be as you imagine - then the thing to do is to imagine and act as though you had faith - as if it is yours - the end imagined.

This is the Law of Liberty. You free yourself and build your faith.

What we voluntarily do will always be the expression of our true belief. Act out the part that you wish to experience, and you will be expressing true faith. "Act as though I were, and I will be," says the Bible.

We shall move mountains - mountains of difficulty, depression, and disappointment - when we are willing to believe that we can, and then not only will mountains be moved, but the whole planet will be redeemed and reformed.

Man cannot save the world until he saves himself. When he saves himself the world is saved.

Know the Truth about your problems. God is Spirit and this is all God so this is all Spirit. Everything has a spiritual cause.

Claim spiritual dominion.

Avoid tenseness, strain, and over-anxiety when you pray. Be relaxed. Expect your prayer to be answered, and act as though you expect it.

Confidence and Assumption.

Say it with feeling - AMEN it is done.

The word Amen means I assume by the God in me this is done.

5 PRACTICAL STEPS

When you set out to solve a problem by means of prayer you should take all the ordinary normal steps you would in addition to the prayer. Wise action must be added to prayer. No worries - you will be guided.

Pray about your difficulty but also claim Divine Guidance, and then take any steps that common sense dictates. You are guided and take that first thought that says do this and do it. Do not second guess. That is your objective side objecting. If you do then pray for divine guidance.

Common sense is common as it is known by all and is sensible. Common sense is itself an expression of Divine Wisdom.

Many people seem to have the idea that taking some "practical" step shows a lack of faith in God and interferes with the power of the prayer.

They ask if that is not trying to serve two masters.

The exact opposite is the case. We all know that an action is but the outer expression of a thought, and that a wise action is the expression of a wise or true thought, and so to take wise steps is the proof that one is thinking rightly, and is, indeed, a part of the answered prayer itself.

Ex. You pray to rid yourself of bedbugs. The first thought you have is to spray for them. God in your heart knows you intimately and he knows you can't get past that these bugs are spiritual. Spray for the bugs. You know God will make them go and make the spray work for you.

Do not simply pray and then sit down and wait for something dramatic to happen. For instance, if you are praying for a job, you should pray for it and then go be happy it is on the way. When you look at positions the right one will pop out at you and if not then sooner or later the right one will come to you in some wonderful way. You don't stop looking for the job waiting for it to dramatically land in your lap. It may dramatically land in your lap but that may come about from meeting someone while you are waiting to be interviewed. You never know.

If you want a healing, pray about it in whatever way you usually find to be best. Some just state the obvious - doctors and their tests are always wrong. I know I am perfectly fine. Done.

This is all spirit and therefore there is no illness. Doctors are a role being played for those who do not have enough faith and see the world objectively. Doctors do not 'cure' you nor their medicines. It is the God in your heart that does this. You just think that pill or protocol is doing it.

Ask yourself if you are living in accordance with the laws of mind, and if not, well up to you whether you like the way you are living life or not. If not, then you must change how you are thinking of the world.

Fear is a mind killer. Fear is present in every problem or difficulty.

If your business is not growing pray. Ask for clarity. Usually the problem is fear and ego in some way - lack of love - and that must be dealt with.

You are not doing a thing other than claiming what you desire. God in your heart and the human imagination are doing it - be grateful you have a wonderful business.

When you pray for guidance or inspiration, it will often come in the form of your own common sense answer to the question. What we call "common sense" is Divine Wisdom taking a particular form.

There is only one being here made up of many and so wisdom often manifests as 'common' sense.

When we have no idea of what to do, your back is against the wall and it appears it is impossible, then that is the time to pray for harmony or for guidance. It will come to you in moments of silence - usually while doing a mundane task or when you first wake up.

6 UNDERSTANDING & FORGIVENESS

There is a big difference between what you really believe and what you think you ought to believe, or what you want to believe. You actually experience what you really believe, be it good or bad. The beliefs that are wrapped around you heart. The responses are automatic.   That is your state of consciousness.

The beliefs wrapped around your heart are self imposed and can be changed and God in your heart will do it for you. If you go within and forgive others for showing you whatever it is you did not like and accept that God is taking care of it then understanding comes to you. God changes how you see it. God changes them.

When there are misunderstandings then things are not in harmony and judging has happened. Forgive, pray for harmony and an ocean of Divine Love washes it all away. Your perceptions will change.

If you are holding grudges, maligning others, etc., then you have given your power to the outside world and it is time to take it back. Forgiveness does this. Forgiveness is an act of love. Forgiveness wipes the slate clean.

You forgive others for showing you what you disliked about them and thank the son, Jesus/Human Imagination and the Father -

God/Consciousness in your heart for changing how you see something or someone - then it is done and think of it no more.

Ex. If you think Tom is a jerk then no matter what comes out of his mouth or what he does you will perceive him being a jerk even while he says please and thank you. You will see and hear it as sarcastic or condescending talk.

You forgive Tom . I forgive Tom for showing me he can be sarcastic and ugly and rude. I know he is not really like that. Thank you Jesus for taking care of this. I know you hear me Father. I know you always hear me and you always say yes. Thank you. AMEN.

Amen means by God it is done. Now you drop it and think of the ugly no more when/if you think of Tom.

Now you go outside and see Tom. Now he says the same kind of things but you hear it differently. Tom has not changed. The way you perceive Tom has changed.

You do not have to struggle with changing how you see, what you believe, of someone or something. Forgive and let God do it for you.

Now some learn the law of liberty - imagination creates reality - and use it over and over and have no problem just doing that to shape a great life and they assume it will be and so it will be.

However, the law of liberty is to save you from yourself when you get yourself into trouble and it looks hopeless. You have made a real mess of it. We all do it but it is not for you to use in shaping your life. It's ok if you do but eventually God will make you face your fears in dreams and visions. Eventually you will forgive them all or have more pain and suffering until you learn and do forgive.

When you experience enough conscious manifestation you come to know it in your heart that you can do this no problem. The Law of Liberty helps you do this. This is how you build faith to take you up the ladder of consciousness and obtaining an understanding that leads to assumption.

Man must claim and command as he has dominion over all here. He is the one learning to think so he thinks and it comes to be on the screen of time and space. You experience what you think in some way and should walk away with a lesson learned instead of blame and guilt.

Some use the law of liberty and see others as stuffed animals or tin soldiers they are pushing around. These are the ones that will have to face themselves sooner or later as they assume no one on the outside can harm them and they can't when that is wrapped around your heart. But that is really an objective way to see it and that must be changed in the end.

It is not much use saying that you know that a thing will not hurt you if you only know it in your head - intellectually. It has to be a knowing - written on your heart.

It is not enough to say that you will be all right, unless you believe it in your heart.

It is not enough to say that God will take care of you unless you realize, understand, and believe and therefore assume what you are saying is in your heart - at the very least to a small degree. Sincere. If you don't believe it - even one grain of it - sincerely - then that is what is on your heart and it must be removed to move forward.

You are 'praying' all the time. Therefore you manifest all the time so you will have your desires with prayer but that rise in consciousness where there is only harmony between you and the rest of the world will remain beyond your reach without forgiveness. Forgiveness brings understanding and clarity.

The sole object of prayer is to increase your knowledge of the truth which you already accept; namely that God can and will protect you from all harm, and that fear and misunderstanding have no power when you yourself do not give it to them. You are the operator - you have dominion over all.

Understanding is knowledge that God - a whole and pure consciousness - is in your heart literally and is absolutely real to you. If you can KNOW the Presence of God is within you - in your heart - and all is well then where previously you were thinking of a damaged organ, for instance, the organ in question will begin to heal.

It makes no difference whether you are praying for yourself or for someone else, or how far away the other person may be. The law of One is the same. In practice most people find it easier to heal someone else in this way than themselves.

What you give you get so you will heal as well if this is done for another.

The understanding of God is, of course, a matter of layers of consciousness. With a comfortable degree of understanding a healing will be instantaneous. With a lesser degree it will follow a little later. With lesser degree you keep it up until satisfaction - the healing - has been achieved.

With each conscious manifestation a layer is torn off the heart.

You do it for self or others day after day and you die daily, you are building that faith up to assumption with understanding.

As we progress in Truth and come to understand God in our hearts then we find that it becomes almost instantaneous and in many cases it is instant. The number of prayers required to remove it -

forgiveness and acceptance it is yours - becomes less and less until all prayers become an assumption.

It is not how many times it is done - it is when understanding is achieved that it is done.

7 HOW TO GO TO SILENCE EASILY

Many are encouraged to meditate but it is not what is asked for in the Bible. The Bible asks for one tenth of your time to silence. It asks for you to praise the God in your heart and mind and the one in all men's hearts and minds. It says call upon the name of God and it shall be yours. Claim it as if it is yours and it is yours.

When you go to silence you are shutting up the consciousness in your head and going to the one your heart and just hanging. Being silent.

It only takes a moment to do this and we all do it naturally.

Go sit and have a smoke or a drink.

Do a mundane task that requires no thinking to perform it. You begin the task and once into the task you are in silence.

Sit in a comfy chair and if thoughts come up just say nothing to see here move along just a thought until you achieve silence.

Relax and be silent. Now the stage is set for successful prayer. All prayer is a divine activity and must show itself to you.

Say it and mean it and it will be.

8 MEDITATION

Mediation is prayer where think upon something with all your attention.

Going to silence is the key as that is hushing up the consciousness that is learning how to think and going to the one that is guiding all.

There is no more powerful form of prayer than meditation. It is the Practice of the Presence of God in its most effective form, and is the quickest way out of sin, sickness, and chaos.

Many people have this idea that they cannot meditate or need some sort of guided meditation. Now, the truth is that everyone can and does meditate. You do it all the time.

For example thousands of people meditate deeply upon the subject of baseball during the season, without realizing what they are doing.

Ex. Joe gets up in the morning, picks up his life where he left it before going to sleep; goes down to breakfast and talks about family matters. At the bus stop he reads a paper, reads some of the headings on the front page. Then the bus arrives. He finds a seat, and goes to the sports section and goes to the baseball page. Here he reads stories about baseball teams for ten or fifteen minutes, and now a change takes place. He becomes absorbed in what he is reading; all other subjects fade out of his mind. Home and business troubles, politics, crime, all are forgotten. He lays down the paper and becomes lost in the contemplation of his subject - baseball. In his mind he criticizes the management of his favorite team.

Possibly he thinks of certain changes which he would like to see made in the rules of the game - an armchair manager - and much more along the same lines. The next thing he knows, thirty or forty minutes have passed, and he has arrived at his destination.

That is an example of an excellent meditation except that it has been about baseball instead of about Divine things. This man read about his subject for ten or fifteen minutes and this got him away from the general stream of thought of a day in the life. Having done this, he proceeded to ponder about his subject until he became absorbed in it and so his technique was perfect.

Imitate him, except you read a spiritual book for ten or fifteen minutes, and think about God, the aspects of Love and Life and God and to think about your spiritual self, think about the Truth of Being in any shape or form, you will have made a wonderful meditation too. If you do this you cannot fail to achieve remarkable results.

9 IN TIMES OF DANGER

In times of danger, the best prayer is to be aware of the protecting power of God's Love. God and his Son are you sword and shield and they are with you always.

Where the danger is immediate, a short prayer, like God is here or God is with me, will work. The urgency of the problem - that strong emotion - gives more spiritual weight to the prayer. There have been many cases where someone has slipped or tripped, and this simple prayer has brought them out unharmed.

Ex. You are stopped in traffic. You look in the rear view mirror and see a car going too fast behind you. You know they are going to hit you. You say "God is helping me; God is with me and God is helping me now!" and that car hits you but you are unhurt and can drive off. Perhaps a torn bumper but all is well.

In times of what seems impending danger where there is time to pray, the 91st Psalm should be used, over and over, if need be.

This psalm covers all sorts of situations and is summed up in the thought,

"He shall give his angels charge over thee."

You really do have an angel on your shoulder - in your head and in your heart.

Psalm 91 Assurance of God's Protection

1 He who dwells in the shelter of the Most High, who abides in the shadow of the Almighty,

2 will say to the LORD, "My refuge and my fortress; my God, in whom I trust."

3 For he will deliver you from the snare of the fowler and from the deadly pestilence;

4 he will cover you with his pinions, and under his wings you will find refuge; his faithfulness is a shield and buckler.

5 You will not fear the terror of the night, nor the arrow that flies by day,

6 nor the pestilence that stalks in darkness, nor the destruction that wastes at noonday.A thousand may fall at your side, ten thousand at your right hand; but it will not come near you.

8 You will only look with your eyes and see the recompense of the wicked.

9 Because you have made the LORD your refuge,the Most High your habitation,

10 no evil shall befall you, no scourge come near your tent. For he will give his angels charge of you to guard you in all your ways.

12 On their hands they will bear you up, lest you dash your foot against a stone.

13 You will tread on the lion and the adder, the young lion and the serpent you will trample under foot.

14 Because he cleaves to me in love, I will deliver him; I will protect him, because he knows my name.

15 When he calls to me, I will answer him; I will be with him in trouble, I will rescue him and honor him.

16 With long life I will satisfy him, and show him my salvation.

64

WORKS CITED

Abarim Publications - https://www.abarim-publications.com/Meaning/Abraham.html

The Bible - Revised Standard Version

Fox, Emmett - all his work is available at Amazon and various book sellers throughout the world

J. Andrew Armour M.D.,Ph.D.- Intrinsic Cardiac Neurons - https://onlinelibrary.wiley.com/doi/abs/10.1111/j.1540-8167.1991.tb01330.x

Merriam-Webster Dictionary, https://www.merriam-webster.com/

Neville Goddard - all his work is available in the public domain

ABOUT THE AUTHOR

Rita Cragwall is an expert on crowd psychology, markets, cooking, family, the Bible, and the 12 Laws of Mind. She is an expert at many things as we all are in this life. She is a teacher and she teaches others how to fish, how to live life, rather than survive it. She loves to share knowledge. She runs a library at Patreon and assists those that support this message with hundreds of blogs, videos and podcasts on how to use the 12 Laws of Mind. She has assisted thousands in their journey to a better life.

It's about helping each other, each one of us individually therefore it's about humanity. Her books are available at Amazon.
https://www.amazon.com/Rita-Cragwall/e/B01BDLZB76
Her library is at Patreon.
https://www.patreon.com/thelawandthepromise
She can be reached at these social media outlets.
Minds - https://www.minds.com/RCragwall
Reddit - https://www.reddit.com/user/RCragwall
Rumble - https://rumble.com/c/c-373445
Gab - https://gab.com/rcragwall
Facebook - https://www.facebook.com/rcragwallfans
LinkedIn - https://www.linkedin.com/in/rcragwall
YouTube -
https://www.youtube.com/channel/UCwieDiJGLpIwr5opqB_g_Y
Q

68

www.ingramcontent.com/pod-product-compliance
Lightning Source LLC
Chambersburg PA
CBHW071949120726
48001CB00005B/2096